The Beginning
of the World

Masahiro Kasuya

THE
PILGRIM
PRESS
Cleveland

In the beginning when God created the heavens and the earth, the earth was a formless void and darkness covered the face of the deep...

Then God said, "Let there be light"

God called the light Day, and the darkness Night.
And there was evening and there was morning, the first day.

And God said, "Let there be a dome in the midst of the waters,
and let it separate the waters from the waters."

God called the dome Sky. And there was evening and there was morning, the second day.

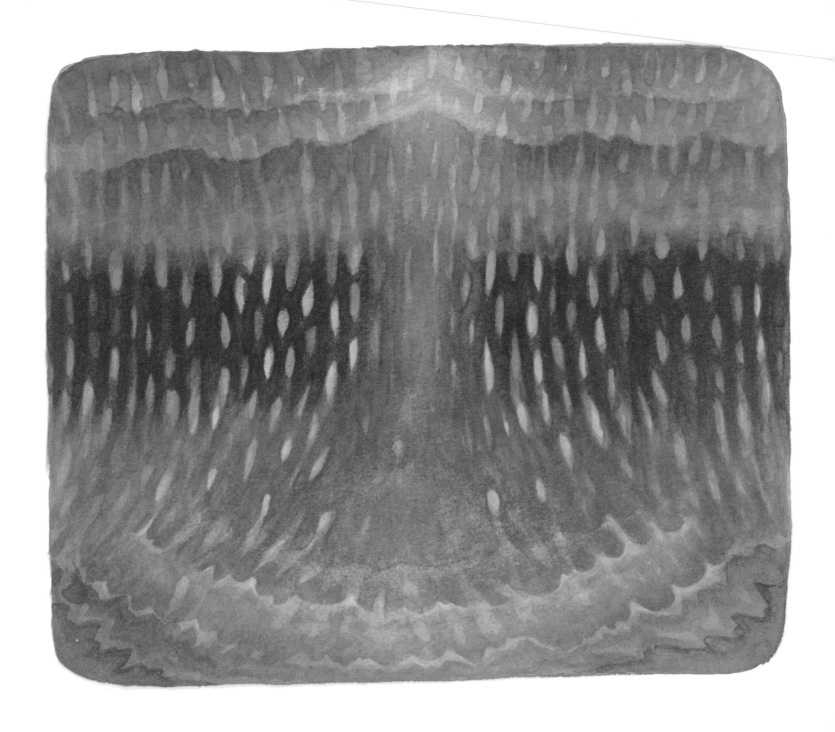

And God said, "Let the waters under the sky be gathered together into one place,
and the dry land appear.

Then God said, "Let the earth put forth vegetation: plants yielding seed, and fruit trees of every kind on earth that bear fruit with the seed in it." And there was evening and there was morning, the third day.

And God said, "Let there be lights in the dome of the sky to separate the day from the night; and let them be for signs and for seasons, and for days and years...

God made the two great lights – the greater light to rule the day
and the lesser light to rule the night – and the stars...
And there was evening and there was morning, the fourth day.

And God said, "Let the waters bring forth swarms of living creatures...

So God created the great sea monsters and every living creature that moves...

So God created…every winged bird of every kind…God blessed them, saying,
"Be fruitful and multiply and fill the waters in the seas, and let birds multiply on the earth."

And there was evening and there was morning, the fifth day.

And God said, "Let the earth bring forth living creatures of every kind: cattle and creeping things and wild animals of the earth of every kind."

And God saw that it was good.

Then God said, "Let us make humankind in our image, according to our likeness...
See, I have given you every plant yielding seed that is upon the face of all the earth,

and every tree with seed in its fruit; you shall have them for food...
And there was evening and there was morning, the sixth day.

Thus the heavens and the earth were finished, and all their multitude.

So God blessed the seventh day and hallowed it, because on it God rested from all the work that God had done in creation.

Many thousands of years passed. The people multiplied

all over the world and built themselves houses.

New people are being born everyday,

And God gives each person a special face—yours too.

THE BEGINNING OF THE WORLD

English texts are Biblical quotations from the
New Revised Standard Version of the Bible,
© 1989 by the Division of Christian Education of the
National Council of Churches of Christ in the U.S.A.,
and used by permission.
Adapted for inclusivity.
Selection and arrangement © 2002 The Pilgrim Press
700 Prospect Avenue
Cleveland, Ohio 44115-1100 U.S.A.
pilgrimpress.com
All rights reserved.
Illustration © Masahiro Kasuya.
Original Japanese Text © Akiko Kageyama
Original Japanese Edition "Kamisamano otsukurininatta sekai" published
in 1979 by Shiko-Sha., Co., Ltd.. Tokyo, Japan.
Printed in China
07 06 05 04 03 02   5 4 3 2 1
ISBN 0-8298-1512-0